INTRODUCTION

TODAY MOST OF US LIVE IN A MIXED-RACE SOCIETY, WHICH REPRESENTS A RANGE OF DIFFERENT PEOPLES, CULTURES AND BELIEFS.

This variety of cultures enriches all of our lives. Unfortunately, it also means that most of us will come into contact with racism and prejudice.

This book will help you to find out more about racism, the different ways in which people can be racist, and the reasons for their behaviour. Each chapter introduces a different aspect of the subject, illustrated by a continuing storyline. The characters in the story have to deal with situations which many of you may experience yourselves. After each episode, we stop and look at the issues raised, and widen out the discussion. By the end, you should know more about racism, how it affects people's lives, and what can be done to challenge it.

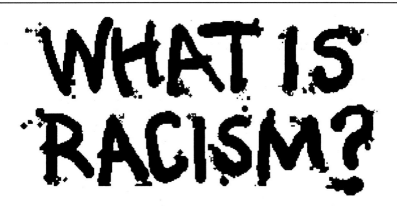

WHAT IS RACISM?

THERE ARE OVER FIVE BILLION PEOPLE IN THE WORLD, LIVING IN OVER 200 COUNTRIES. WE BELONG TO DIFFERENT RACES, CULTURES AND RELIGIONS.

Many people believe that these differences are there to be shared and celebrated. Some people, however, use them as an excuse to treat certain people as inferior in some way.

Racism exists in all races and cultures. It is more than just believing your own race to be better than someone else's. It is treating people differently and unfairly simply because they belong to another race. Racists usually target those who are in the minority in society, but not always. In South Africa a relatively small white population ruled the black majority for hundreds of years. Racism is anything said or done to harm, ridicule or disadvantage someone from another race.

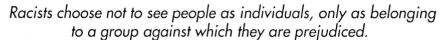

Racists choose not to see people as individuals, only as belonging to a group against which they are prejudiced.

Most racist beliefs are not founded on fact.
Terry is repeating comments he has heard, which are based on mistrust or hatred, not on evidence. He knows little about the Smart family personally. He is prejudiced against all black people, because of lies and half-truths he has been told by others. Information which misleads people on purpose into believing something which may not be true is called "propaganda". Terry has been listening to racist propaganda.

Terry is stereotyping black people.
He is using generalisations to apply to a whole group of people. This is like saying that all boys like to play football, or all girls play with dolls. Comments such as these may be true for some people, but they do not apply to everyone. This kind of stereotyping helps racists, because it refuses to see people as individuals. Racist stereotypes are usually very negative. The picture above reinforces negative images of the black "slave" and white "master".

By jumping to conclusions, as Terry has done, you may miss out on what other people have to offer.
You don't have to like everybody – each person has strengths and weaknesses. Being non-racist does not mean that you cannot dislike or disagree with someone of a different race to your own. But your judgement should be based on what you find out about each particular person. It is never helpful to prejudge anybody. This only sets up barriers between you and others, before you even get to know them.

DIFFERENT KINDS OF RACISM

THE MOST OBVIOUS TYPE OF RACISM OCCURS WHEN PEOPLE ARE SINGLED OUT BECAUSE OF THE COLOUR OF THEIR SKIN. BUT THIS IS NOT THE ONLY KIND.

Racists may also pick on people because they come from a different country or culture, or belong to a different religion.
Racism takes many different forms. You may have seen racists calling people rude names, or making fun of the way they dress or the food they eat. Sometimes racists try to make others feel small or unwanted. They might prevent someone from taking part in an activity, and try to make others do the same. More and more racist attacks involve violence, and these can often be very serious indeed.

Racism is not always obvious. Sometimes plausible excuses are given to disguise a racist action. For instance, white parents may move their child from a mixed-race school, saying the new school will offer the child a better education. Their real reason might be that they do not want their child mixing with children from other cultures. Some racist acts may seem minor, compared to others, but this does not make them any more acceptable. All kinds of racism are wrong.

Some people make no attempt to mix with others from different cultures. They might ignore them completely, treating them as if they didn't exist.

▽ Next day, as Jake, Natalie and her friend Usha waited for a bus, Terry and Mick appeared.

IF IT ISN'T BLACKIE AND PAKI. ARE THESE TWO BOTHERING YOU, JAKE?

NO, WE WERE JUST TALKING, THAT'S ALL.

WELL DON'T GET TOO CLOSE, JEW BOY, YOU NEVER KNOW WHAT YOU MIGHT CATCH.

VERY FUNNY. WHY DON'T YOU LEAVE US ALONE?

▽ Jake and Natalie got off at the same stop.

▽ On the way home...

DON'T LET THEM GET TO YOU. THAT'S WHAT THEY WANT.

TERRY'S O.K. REALLY. HE WAS JUST SHOWING OFF.

WAIT TILL HE REALLY STARTS PICKING ON YOU FOR BEING JEWISH. THEN YOU'LL KNOW HOW IT FEELS.

THEY'RE HORRID. I HATE THEM ALL.

WHAT WERE YOU DOING WITH HIM?

WE CAUGHT THE SAME BUS. WHAT ARE YOU IN SUCH A MOOD ABOUT?

THEY SAID I DIDN'T HAVE ENOUGH EXPERIENCE. BUT I KNOW IT'S BECAUSE I'M BLACK.

△ Natalie's brother Winston had been for a job interview and had been turned down.

Do you think Winston may be right?

Terry knows that he can hurt the girls' feelings by calling them names.

Racists like to label people, as another way of denying them their individuality. They use words which they know will offend. These words may sound very mild, but they can still be deeply hurtful. It is important to use language carefully, and be aware of the effect your words may have. Wherever possible, avoid using words to label people. The way you express your ideas will show respect or disrespect for other people's cultures.

Winston was not pleased to see Natalie with Jake.

When two people from different ethnic backgrounds become friends, their families and others close to them may have very strong views about the situation. They may not want the relationship to continue, particularly if it becomes intimate. This is another form of prejudice. There can be religious or cultural differences to cope with, but these need not be a barrier. Many people enjoy successful mixed-race relationships.

Children from mixed-race families sometimes face special problems.

Some children have one black parent and one white one. This may make them the targets of racism from both black and white people.

Winston feels he didn't get the job because he is black.

Racial discrimination is when someone is disadvantaged because of their race, culture or religion. It is against the law in many countries to discriminate in this way. After all, the colour of a person's skin has nothing to do with his or her ability to do a particular job. Unfortunately, many organisations find ways around the law. If a firm has managers or workers with racist views, it can also be very difficult for a person such as Winston to gain promotion.

WHY ARE PEOPLE RACIST?

RACISM IS OFTEN BASED ON IGNORANCE AND FEAR OF ANYTHING UNFAMILIAR. INSTEAD OF FINDING OUT ABOUT OTHER CULTURES, RACISTS CHOOSE TO HATE OR DESPISE ANYONE WHO IS DIFFERENT.

People are not born racist. Their views develop as they grow up.
Some young people live in a situation where family or friends are racist. They may believe that racism is normal and acceptable, and adopt the same ideas themselves. Racists may see other cultures as a threat to their own. Many claim to be acting for the good of their country, to keep their own race "pure" – separate and distinct from others. They view anyone of a different race, even those born in the same country, as an outsider. Sticking together and sharing ideas with people who think in the same way reinforces this kind of prejudice.

Some racism is caused by a desire to gain or maintain advantage over others. If one section of a community has an advantage over another section, members of the advantaged group may wish to hold on to their privilege or power. They may not want the situation to become more equal.

Under the aparteid system in South Africa black and white people were kept separate on buses and trains, in cinemas and even on park benches.

▽ Terry's family went to his cousin Jackie's house.

▽ Jackie's parents welcomed them to the barbecue. Jackie was in Terry's class at school.

▷ Everyone was embarrassed by their remarks.

▽ The gang began to laugh.

△ Jackie walked away in disgust.

△ Back at school, Terry and Mick teased Natalie.

11

Do you think Jake should have done something to stop the gang?

People often have very strong views about the area they live in.

Mr Stoddard's remarks are based on the idea that different cultures should not mix with one another. In some countries this has even led to separation of different groups of people. Under the system of "apartheid", black South Africans were not allowed to live in the same town, use the same public transport or the same beach as white people. When a group of people is confined to one area in this way, the neighbourhood is called a "ghetto".

It can be great fun to share experiences with a group of friends.

Gangs like Terry's, though, can cause trouble. It is very easy in a gang situation to be swept along by what the gang is doing, even if you feel you do not want to take part. It can be hard to speak out against what everyone else is saying. Racists often use this to their advantage. Some racist attacks are carried out by mobs of people. In the heat of the moment, some may not realise what they are doing, or may go further than they intended.

Jake could have spoken up for Natalie, but chose to stay silent.

Racists often act in the way they do because they are allowed to get away with it. They often rely on people being afraid to challenge them. If those around them refused to accept their behaviour, they might think twice about continuing. Ignoring racism only helps it to develop. Silence is no answer, because if you don't speak out against racism you will appear to be going along with it.

THE EFFECTS OF RACISM

RACISM IS SOMETHING THAT AFFECTS EVERYBODY.

Racists miss the opportunity to learn about other cultures and about people as individuals. Those who are being victimised may become racist back, as a way of dealing with what is happening.

If you are being picked on by racists, you might become lonely and depressed. You might try to avoid situations where racism could occur, and pretend to be ill, or play truant from school. If you are experiencing threats or violence, you might become scared to leave the safety of home. The worry could make it difficult to sleep properly, and your work might suffer.

Sometimes people who are experiencing racism start to accept it as a way of life, and expect racist incidents to continue. They might even think that they are in some way to blame for the situation. If you are always being told that you are inferior, you may eventually start to believe that this is so. Sometimes racism leads to violence. It may result in fights between individuals or "rival" gangs, or even worse, in war.

Racist views have been the cause of wars, both between different countries and between groups of people in the same country.

▽ It was 8.15 and Natalie still had not come down for breakfast.

NATALIE, WHAT ARE YOU DOING? WHY AREN'T YOU DRESSED?

▽ There was no reply. Janet Smart went upstairs to Natalie's room.

NATALIE, YOU'RE GOING TO BE LATE FOR SCHOOL.

▽ Suddenly Natalie began to cry. She told her mum about the racist bullying.

YOU PROMISED THINGS WOULD BE DIFFERENT HERE.

▽ Mrs Smart told Natalie she couldn't help if she didn't know who was responsible.

IS IT JAKE? I'VE SEEN HIM PLAYING WITH TERRY STODDARD. THE STODDARDS LIKE CAUSING TROUBLE.

WE HOPED THEY WOULD BE. WHO IS IT WHO'S SAYING THINGS?

I DAREN'T TELL YOU, MUM. I'M AFRAID.

SHE'S BEGINING TO THINK IT'S HER OWN FAULT. WHAT ARE WE GOING TO DO?

That evening...

FIRST WINSTON AND NOW NATALIE. IT'S SO UNFAIR.

I KNOW. IT LOOKS LIKE MOVING HASN'T SOLVED ANYTHING.

I DON'T KNOW. BUT WE'RE NOT GOING TO PUT UP WITH IT ANY MORE.

△ The Smarts had decided to move after Winston was beaten up on his way home.

What do you think the Smarts should do?

15

The way we feel about ourselves is influenced by the way others treat us. Many racists are aware of this. Like Terry, they use racism to frighten and ridicule people, even to the point where they begin to doubt their own worth. Racists might deny you the right to succeed, by making you believe you do not deserve success. Or they may make think that you are not good at something. This has the effect of lowering your expectations of yourself, and may prevent you from achieving as much as you could have otherwise.

The Smart family have been the targets of racism in the past. They had hoped that a move to a new house would help. Sometimes a problem can become so bad that it seems running away from it is the only answer. But as Natalie is finding out, it is not always possible to escape racism in this way. Sometimes situations have to be faced up to, however difficult that may be.

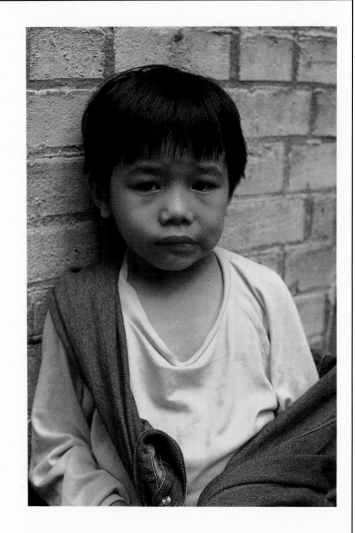

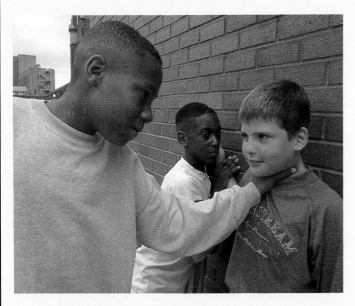

Terry and his gang are bullies. Racism is a form of bullying, and you know that bullying is always wrong. Like many bullies, racists may attempt to excuse their behaviour by saying that it is "just a bit of fun". If you have ever been bullied, for any reason, you will understand how serious bullying is, and the effect it can have on your self-esteem. Nobody should have to put up with bullying or racism. It is essential to remember that you are in the right, and it is the racists who are at fault.

HIDDEN RACISM

SOME PEOPLE FIND WAYS TO COVER UP RACIST ACTIONS. OTHERS, HOWEVER, MAY NOT EVEN EVEN REALISE THAT THEY ARE BEING RACIST.

Hidden racism is difficult to challenge, because no-one seems to be purposely acting in a racist way, and no-one appears to be directly affected. But hidden racism can be just as damaging as open racism. Hidden racism helps to develop ideas that are stereotyped and inaccurate. The way races are shown in books and on TV is often incorrect. In "Wild West" films, "Indians" – native Americans – are usually shown as savages. In reality, many tribes were non-violent, and only fought to protect their land. A news item on TV or in a newspaper may mention a person's colour in connection with a story, even though it is completely irrelevant. If the story happens to concern a crime, this can set up a negative idea in the mind of the person reading or watching. People in countries where there is famine are presented as helpless and in need of our pity. These images can take away people's dignity, and encourage us to believe all those in developing countries need help. Hidden racism is danger-ous. It is important never to take for granted what you see or hear. Only judge a situation once you have a full picture of it.

Images such as the loyal black servant may become so familiar that we forget to question whether they are right or wrong.

▽ Without telling Natalie, the Smarts went to see the headteacher, Mr Samuels.

THIS IS VERY SERIOUS. WE DON'T TOLERATE RACISM AT THIS SCHOOL.

WE HAVE STRICT RULES TO MAKE CERTAIN EVERYONE IS TREATED EQUALLY. ANY REPORTS OF RACISM ARE DEALT WITH SEVERELY.

△ Mr Samuels told the Smarts what the school did to stop racism.

THERE ARE MANY DIFFERENT CULTURES WITHIN THE SCHOOL. WE TRY TO CELEBRATE THEM ALL.

IT ALL SOUNDS VERY NICE. BUT WE STILL HAVE A PROBLEM.

▷ Mr Samuels promised he would try to sort out the issue.

▽ Next day Janet Smart met Liz Friedman.

HOW ARE YOU SETTLING IN?

OK, EXCEPT FOR SOME PROBLEMS NATALIE'S HAVING AT SCHOOL.

▽ Janet told Liz about the racism, and that she thought Jake might be involved.

I'M SURE YOU'RE WRONG. JAKE WOULDN'T DO ANYTHING LIKE THAT.

I THINK HE'S BEING INFLUENCED BY TERRY STODDARD.

JAKE KNOWS I WON'T STAND FOR RACISM. WE'RE JEWISH, MRS SMART— WE'VE HAD OUR SHARE OF RACIST COMMENTS.

IT'S DIFFERENT FOR YOU. YOU'RE STILL WHITE.

What do you think Mrs Smart means?

Like Natalie's school, many organisations today have equal opportunities policies. These are meant to make sure that nobody is discriminated against because of their colour, gender, disability, class, religious beliefs, age or sexuality. Just having the policy, however, may not always be enough to prevent discrimination. To be effective in stopping racism, everybody must be aware of the policy and agree to stick to its rules. There must also be strict procedures to deal with anyone who breaks these rules.

Making sure all cultures are positively represented in society is essential in challenging racism.

However, it is important that it is a true representation. Many feel that when different races are shown in the media, it often amounts to only a token gesture. You may have seen films where there is one "token" black character amongst a large number of white ones. Tokenism is not effective in challenging racism, and may even add to it.

Racists choose to focus on differences rather than connections and similarities. Most racists target anyone whom they see as different. As Mrs Smart has pointed out, however, some differences are more obvious than others. For instance, a racist may not be able to tell if you are Jewish simply by looking at you. Fear of racial abuse may make some people try to hide or deny their race or religion. This is another kind of hidden racism. Your own culture is something you should be able to be proud of.

THE HISTORY OF RACISM

THROUGHOUT HISTORY, BILLIONS OF PEOPLE HAVE SUFFERED AND DIED AS A RESULT OF PREJUDICE AND HATRED.

Racism has affected people both as individuals and as groups. Most examples of racism involving individuals have gone unrecorded. They were never reported or written down.

Over the last 500 years, much racism has been a result of the colonies established by white Europeans in Africa, Asia, the Americas and Australia. European settlers claimed the land and resources of these countries for themselves and their own nations. History books often talk about the discovery of new lands, as though they did not exist before they were visited by white explorers. The native inhabitants found their rights and lands taken from them. Europeans even enslaved millions of Africans and sold them as servants and cheap labour for the plantations of North America. Slavery was not finally abolished in Britain and the United States until the mid-1800s.

This century has also seen great cruelty and suffering caused by racism. Even until the 1990s black South Africans were ruled under the apartheid system by white people descended from European settlers. During the 1930s and 40s Nazi Germany persecuted Jewish people and sent millions of Jews to concentration camps. Six million Jews were murdered by the Nazis.

White people regarded black slaves as their personal property and often treated them badly.

▽ That evening Jake's mum confronted him.

AND SAID NOTHING. THAT'S AS BAD AS JOINING IN.

IT WAS TERRY, REALLY. I JUST HAPPENED TO BE THERE.

I DIDN'T MEAN ANY HARM.

YOU OF ALL PEOPLE SHOULD KNOW HOW DANGEROUS RACISM IS.

◁ When they were his age, Jake's grandparents had had to leave Austria when the Nazis took over.

▽ Jake had heard about this before, but was just beginning to understand fully.

THEY WERE LUCKY. MILLIONS OF JEWS WERE KILLED. IF ORDINARY GERMANS HAD DONE SOMETHING TO TRY TO STOP THE NAZIS, MANY OF THOSE PEOPLE MIGHT NOT HAVE DIED.

IT WASN'T EASY ONCE THEY GOT TO THIS COUNTRY, EITHER. THEY WERE TREATED AS SECOND CLASS CITIZENS. PEOPLE WERE VERY RACIST.

▷ Jake realised the devastating effect racism can have on people's lives.

I'LL APOLOGISE TO NATALIE. I SHOULD HAVE DONE SOME-THING.

Although Jake had heard about the events of World War II before, he is beginning to realise the true horror of what happened.

The Nazis blamed Jewish people for the problems of their society. Jews were thrown out of their homes and had their property taken away. Some, like the children shown right, escaped to Britain. But many Jews were sent to concentration camps, where millions died. Despite all the evidence, there are still groups of racists today, who try to deny that these events, known as the holocaust, ever happened. This is yet another example of racism.

Jake now knows that none of us must ever forget the terrible consequences of racism.

At the same time, it is not helpful to go on blaming new generations of people for the actions of their parents or grandparents. You cannot change what has happened in the past. Racism relies on people continuing to be prejudiced against one another. It can only be stopped by putting aside grudges and resentments and talking openly.

Jake's grandparents escaped from the Nazis, but met a different kind of prejudice when they came to Britain.

Like other groups of people moving to new countries, they had no choice but to accept the poorly-paid work that nobody else wanted to do. In the past some countries have even encouraged people to leave their homeland for this reason. For example, in the 1950s West Indians moved to Britain and did low-paid work. Then when jobs became harder to find, these immigrants were resented for having work, whilst those born in the country had none.

RACISM TODAY

STUDYING HISTORY CAN HELP US TO LEARN FROM THE MISTAKES THAT OTHERS HAVE MADE IN THE PAST. UNFORTUNATELY, THIS DOES NOT ALWAYS PREVENT US FROM REPEATING THEM.

In some countries today, the situation has improved for those who were the target of racism and prejudice. However, this has often happened too slowly, and not always effectively.

In many countries minority groups now have full rights as citizens, and racism is illegal. But laws do not necessarily change people's attitudes, and racist acts continue to happen. There have been some recent dramatic changes. Apartheid has now been abolished in South Africa, and black people have the right to vote for the government. But in many countries racism continues to cause war and suffering. Following the break-up of Yugoslavia, for example, thousands have been killed in racial conflict, and millions more are refugees. In Rwanda in east Africa, one million people have died in a racial fight for power. Today racism is more widely recognised than in the past. It is still a major problem which affects the whole of society.

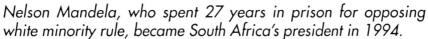

Nelson Mandela, who spent 27 years in prison for opposing white minority rule, became South Africa's president in 1994.

▷ Mr Samuels said a parent complained of racism.

I'LL BET IT WAS THAT NATALIE'S MUM AND DAD.

SO WHAT? I WOULDN'T BLAME THEM.

▽ In class, the teacher introduced a new girl.

IRINA'S JUST JOINED THE SCHOOL. SHE'S FROM BOSNIA, AND DOESN'T SPEAK OUR LANGUAGE YET.

SHE MUST BE THICK IF SHE DOESN'T SPEAK ENGLISH.

MAYUMI DIDN'T SPEAK ENGLISH TWO YEARS AGO, AND SHE'S MUCH CLEVERER THAN YOU.

▽ The teacher heard what Terry had said.

I'LL BET HER PARENTS HAVEN'T GOT JOBS. YOU KNOW WHO'LL END UP PAYING FOR THEM.

US, AS USUAL.

THAT'S A HORRIBLE THING TO SAY, TERRY.

MY DAD SAYS WE'VE ENOUGH PROBLEMS IN THIS COUNTRY. PEOPLE SHOULDN'T BE ALLOWED IN SO EASILY.

YOUR DAD DOESN'T KNOW WHAT HE'S TALKING ABOUT. IT'S NOT EASY. THERE ARE LOADS OF RULES.

△ The teacher tried to explain the situation, but Terry refused to listen.

TRY TO IMAGINE YOURSELF IN IRINA'S POSITION, TERRY.

How do you think Irina feels?

Irina is a refugee, forced to seek shelter in a new country.

Like many of the millions of refugees in the world today, she has been forced to flee because of racism. Many refugees must leave their homes at short notice because their lives are threatened. Most are forced to abandon everything – family, friends, jobs and possessions. Reaching a new country, they may be shocked and scared because of the violence they have seen, and the dangers and hardships they have experienced.

Terry thinks Irina must be stupid because she cannot speak his language.

As Jackie knows, this is not true. If you were taken to a foreign country, and were unable to communicate, this would not mean that you were any less clever. Learning a new language takes time and effort, as well as intelligence. Some people do not believe that they should have to know another language. Yet they expect others to be able to speak theirs!

In Bosnia (above) and in other countries, ethnic cleansing has been responsible for the deaths of thousands of people.

"Ethnic cleansing" is the term used to describe killing people of a different race or culture and taking over their land. The idea is to ensure that all the people who live in a certain area are of the same race or religion. It is based on the false belief that one race is purer than another.

Terry's father believes that all immigrants are a burden to society. This is not true.

The immigration laws in most countries are very strict. Refugees are not allowed in without a good reason. Some do arrive in their new country with nothing, because they have had to leave everything behind. Others have family or jobs to go to. All must try to begin a new life in a strange country, and need support and under-standing. Being in a new place is often very hard to adjust to. Racism can make the change even more difficult.

CHALLENGING RACISM

THERE IS NO EASY ANSWER TO THE PROBLEM OF RACISM. THE FIRST STEP IN STOPPING IT IS TO UNDERSTAND THAT IT EXISTS AND TO RECOGNISE WHEN IT IS HAPPENING.

Racism is always unacceptable. Some racist acts are more severe than others, but all racism should be challenged.

The way this can be done will vary depending on the situation. You will need to judge when it is best to leave a situation quietly, and when to stand up for yourself. Sometimes it is possible to challenge racism personally. At other times it may be better to involve other people. In many schools young people and adults work together to produce anti-racist policies. Working with others in a group can help to improve things. Adults may urge politicians to press for anti-racist laws, and support political candidates who share their views. Many companies, when advertising for jobs, try to attract applications from ethnic minorities. In many countries, the government recognises racism as being wrong, and has made laws to protect people's rights. Some people believe these laws need to be enforced more strongly. Racism has a negative effect on everyone's life. By opposing it at every opportunity, we can show that we value all members of society.

One way of challenging racism is to organise marches to protest against discrimination.

▽ At lunchtime, Jake volunteered to help look after Irina. Terry and Mick went over to them.

SIDING WITH THE ENEMY, JEW BOY?

THERE ARE NO ENEMIES, JUST IGNORANT PEOPLE LIKE YOU AND YOUR DAD.

WE'RE ALL DIFFERENT, TERRY. WE'RE JUST GLAD WE'RE NOT THE SAME AS YOU.

▽ Terry lashed out at Jake.

YOU MAKE ME SICK. YOU'RE NO DIFFERENT THAN THEY ARE.

I'M NOT GOING TO FIGHT YOU.

▽ Terry ran off as the teacher approached.

△ Everyone started to laugh at Terry, even Mick.

▽ After school, Jake apologised to Natalie.

I'LL GET MY GANG ONTO YOU.

LEAVE HIM ALONE.

ALL YOU KNOW HOW TO DO IS HIT PEOPLE.

I WAS STUPID TO LISTEN TO TERRY. DO YOU WANT TO WALK WITH ME TO THE BUS?

I CAN'T. I'M MEETING MUM IN TOWN.

▽ Her mum was late. As Natalie waited, she suddenly saw Terry and Mick coming towards her.

I HAD TO SEE MR. SAMUELS TODAY, BECAUSE OF YOU AND YOUR FAMILY. I MIGHT BE SUSPENDED.

I DIDN'T TELL MY PARENTS IT WAS YOU. I WISH I HAD NOW.

△ The boys saw Mrs Smart approaching, and ran off.

▷ Mrs Smart told Natalie she was late because of a phone call from the headteacher.

▷ Several people had reported Terry. Mr Samuels wanted Natalie to tell what she knew.

▽ The school held a fete at the end of each year.

It is important not to judge people by what others tell you. As Jake has learned, you need to make up your own mind, and not be influenced by other people's opinions. It takes time to get to know someone. Making assumptions and jumping to conclusions about people will not help. It only gets in the way of a possible friendship or relationship.

Ignoring racism will not make it go away.
Natalie had hoped that Terry and his gang would stop their racist abuse. In the end she and Jake had to confront them and stand up for themselves. If racist bullies are allowed to get away with their behaviour, they will continue to harass others. If they are not challenged, their confidence may grow. Eventually, they might turn to more serious or violent forms of racism.

Many racist attacks have involved violence. But as Jake knows, reacting to violence with more violence will solve nothing.
Often a violent response makes a situation worse. It is more effective to challenge racism by discussing differences and similarities between people. Discussion can often show that we have many things in common. And instead of being afraid of our differences, we can share and enjoy them.

WHAT CAN WE DO?

HAVING READ THIS BOOK, YOU WILL UNDERSTAND MORE ABOUT HOW RACISM AFFECTS EVERYONE'S LIVES.

You will know that you should never ignore racism, and how important it is to consider the best way of handling it effectively. Judge each situation carefully. If you are personally being subjected to racist abuse, you will need to decide whether you can deal with the situation alone, or whether you should involve others to help you to challenge it. Racists need help too, particularly in recognising their racism and understanding that it is unacceptable. If you have ever been racist, it might be worthwhile to think about why you acted the way you did. It may help to think about the effect your action had on the other person's well-being. Most of us have absorbed racist messages at some point in our lives. Knowing this enables us to challenge our own ideas and behaviour. This is important, even if we believe ourselves to be non-racist.

Equal Opportunities Commission
Tel: 0161 833 9244
E-mail:
info@eoc.org.uk
Website:
www.eoc.org.uk

Minority Rights Group
379 Brixton Road
London SW9 7DE
Tel: 0207 978 9498
E-mail:
minority.rights@margmail.org
Website:
www.minorityrights.org

ADULTS CAN HELP TOO, BY UNDERSTANDING HOW THEIR WORDS AND ACTIONS CAN INFLUENCE YOUNG PEOPLE.

Children often copy what adults do, and the words they use. If adults around them are racist, they may start to be racist too.
Adults and young people who have read this book together may find it helpful to share their ideas. Sometimes the views of different generations will be very different. Anyone who is experiencing problems with racism or would like to know more about it, can obtain information and support from the organisations listed below.

The Commission for Racial Equality (CRE)– Head Office:
Elliot House
10-12 Allington Street
London SW1E 5EH
Tel: 0207 828 7022
E-mail:
alccon@dircon.co.uk
Website:
www.alcoholconcern.org.uk

CRE Manchester:
40 Blackfriars Street
Manchester
M3 2EG
Tel: 0161 835 5500

CRE Scotland:
45-51 Hanover Street
Edinburgh
EH2 2PJ
Tel: 0131 226 5186

Institute of Race Relations
2-6 Leeke Street
London
WC1X 9HS
Tel: 0207 837 0041
E-mail:
info@irr.org.uk
Website:
www.irr.org.uk

Childline
50 Studd Street
London
N1 0QW
Tel: 0207 239 1000
Childline: 0800 1111
E-mail:
reception@childline.org.uk

Joint Council for the Welfare of Immigrants
115 Old Street
London
EC1V 9JR
Tel: 0207 251 8706

INDEX

Photocredits
All the pictures in this book are by Roger Vlitos apart from pages: 6 middle, 20, 22 top: Hulton Deutsch; 10: Topham Picture Point; 14, 19 top, 23, 25 top, 26, 29 top, 30: Frank Spooner Pictures; 17: Selznick / MGM (courtesy Kobal Collection).